Lengths

&

Breaths

Lee Ranaldo
Photographs by Cynthia Connolly

Water Row Press
Sudbury
2004

Water Row Press
PO Box 438
Sudbury MA 01776
waterrow@aol.com
www.waterrowbooks.com
write for a free catalogue

ISBN 0-934953-79-1
Printed in USA
Book design and typesetting
Henri Hadida (www.henrihadida.com)

Library of Congress Cataloging-in-Publication Data

Ranaldo, Lee.
        Lengths and Breaths / by Lee Ranaldo ;
        photographs by Cynthia Connolly.
     p. cm.
   ISBN 0-934953-79-1 (pbk.)
   I. Title.
   PS3568.A757L46 2004
   811'.54—dc22

2004043006

Dear Charlie,

Sorry it's the same thing again. Next time it'll be Nick Cave motherfucker!

Thanks for everything over the past few months. I hope your 21st is joyous and you have a great year to follow.

My love for ever.

Dom xxx

Breaths

Contents

Lengths

Breaths

Echoes

Fort Meyers Beach, Florida

all of this life strewn before me:
sun visors
books with poems
sneakers on weathered
floorboards
beach towels
magazines, piled high
on tables
today's paper
yesterday's paper
sand dollars
orchids
lawn chairs
buckets, shovels
wrappers
pillows, cushions
shells and sand
waves rolling
night sounding
echoes on the street

all this lies before me,
strewn about:
eyeglasses
chains
the telephone
boxes full of clothes
sandals and
long pants
the quiet teevee
Cody's red shoes
his books
fruit bowls
a clear surface
of dining table
all of it, haphazard,
very real and very
temporary, tonight:
tomorrow we pick up
tomorrow we leave here.

You Tell Me Of Your Day

you tell me of your day
you. tell me.
you smoke, you talk
your eyes open

we talk of many things
and silence stings
we move and we touch
and eyes they open

sometimes i'm wondering
but then i sleep
today i sit
try not to speak

your voice in my ear
and the promise it brings
the girl and the window
keep my eyes open

cars on the street move
the women sway and move away
i move with a feeling
eyes clearly open

Keepers

If I could begin again:
they were all good years
all fine times
with good friends
and women, cars.
So I didn't achieve
an early sophistication
So I remain innocent
somewhat
to this day
Those times
were pure,
real as could be.

Times of insane joy,
with everyone together
when nothing moved
times of *being*

Yes there would be times
to throw out
but I doubt I'd want to
throw away all those days
cavorting around the Volkswagen
in the woods
with Sue and Michael
the radio up loud,
the doors open, blasting
Dancing in the Moonlight
by King Harvest
high and in the sun,
or, for example, walking
a winter's night with
Thom, Jeff and Rob,
one night of many
shooting the shit
kicking an empty
vodka bottle which
we'd found—not drunk—
down Berry Hill Road.
Getting mad at Thom
for smashing it
against a dark wall
downtown
just for kicks.

Or right now even,
doing nothing
listening to wind blowing
through the trees
blow wind blow
hardly thinking at all
watching old movies in my head
and why not?
so true to my depth

I've come this far
things aren't so bad
if I think about it.

re: (Burly)

Said Saler, España

hi it's midnite im in m rm. theres poetry here. dont knowhow t
define it but there is something about these Spanish beach towns
that evokes poetry. like Fire Island w the waves rollin rollin rollin in
all nite n day. palm trees, old adobe brick. poetry Spanish style:
families all out together, eldest included and younglings w soccer-
balls; all out on beach in midday heat or in 10pm tapas bar. food fr
the sea. the sun as substance. *Wow.*

in big handdrawn letters on the outsides of the bldgs here messages
are written. proclamations. love letters.
old cobblestone streets!

Poetry Reveals Itself

poetry reveals
itself
uncovered truths
fleeting thru
shimmering instants
forms resolved
shapes out of shadows
descriptions
space created
ideas imprisoned
in print

Shoulders

for Cody

I feel around my neck now
the warmth and weight
that were yr legs
when you rode me there
high up
about the other heads
deep in my shoulders
smooth to the knee
hands in my hair

that seat reserved for you alone

before I was gone for so long
before the weed you now are
began to surge in earnest
I picture coming home
to yr long lithe limbs
drawing up beside me
yr milk filled bones
more than half my height now
growing into their own right
perhaps our last ride
has already come and gone
without notice
perhaps you have grown
that far without me
in the sun soaked loft
above the dirty little plateau
of city loading docks
where I once lived with you.

Tall Brown Sister

for Melissa

tall brown sister
sliding deep in the well
silver stationwagon eyes
open head sighing
dreaming echoes
beyond conversation
breathing my way
faster now faster
glowing
aching
silent

holding out a hand
building a bridge
fr my shore to yrs
standing unguided
searching then sleeping then
sounding the sky
bell head suspended
yr eyes are fine
and i see you

Second Sight

Second sight
is mine tonight
Every thing that's past this threshold
is now clear
Every mistake stands out
in hard light
Every knot
every misshapen image
every dust mote
all the dirt
Grains of every hour drop
Several sins are mine
Several roads have been left
Several seasons in time
can be seen clearly
in hindsight

Hoarfrost

I put my feet deep in the tracks that you made
Walked behind you off into the wood
We'll know where when we get there, you said
And we both knew we would

High above like spiders
We watched the colors turning brown
Thru the tracks, thru the trees
I took yr hand and we knelt down
We're driftin off with the snow
We're up inside the wind
I catch yr eye as we go
And you come inside again

Waiting for a plan
Dashboard charms in hand
Unroll the maps... and we're gone again...

Wheels paddle wheels paddle movement as we go
Trees passing trees passing signs along the road
A view thru the trees to a couple in the snow
A view thru the trees to a couple standing in the snow

Suddenly the trees were flashing by us
Clouds reflecting fast across your eyes
We turned into a frozen meadow
The wind the only sound
We'll know where when we get there, you said
We'll know where when we get there, you said

Feel This Place

Brooklyn, and the big family
scraggly plants
everywhere
hung out in the sun
Sundays along the sidewalks
talking,
hanging on the patio

feel this place
the pull of this:
the tone of conversations
the expressive tongue
all the children
the wine-drinking
the early morning *bocci* mysteries

this life:
it ends w me
shadowy memories
archaic no longer
whole languages gone
the great big families
of an even dozen children
in washed out pictures
home cooked
almost through
in silent movies
waiting

Now new children
are flowering
the old culture
a dusty shelf
a faded object
almost gone
discarded treasures
black pages
supplanted by
smooth flesh
milk-fed
child-globes.

the modern,
possible age.
who knows what comes next?

19? Feb?

I remember
Mary in the trees
like elm bark oozing sap
The light of day
forever loosing slack
Every day a new route
the world spinning fast
Confusion
setting in
clearing out the room
crawling up my leg
into my mouth

Inlet

a trip on the stairs
the sound of steps
behind
the street, the clouds
the cars
shine
there's air
clear steps ahead
no-one talking
no-one to see
the clouds, the fence
the dogs
an age ends with these

metered moves, each step
the pavement cracked and wet
the bells. the water.
go on and on

the promise and the peace
the kiss and stroke
the days we spent
go on and on

Jasper's Death

foreign coins
dusty silvered keychains
second grade notebooks
locks w/o keys
pants too small and full of meaning

photo after photo
pictures of a life
pictures of your face
as we knew you

pictures of a room
we shared
when time stood still
for a moment
and ev'ry movement
was a slow caress
in the endless brilliance
of bright afternoon
leaves shaking
eyes shining
hands laughing in the air
quieting the world
—together!

sharing a slip
down a green grass strip
before the end comes
quickening away.

Richard

Richard:
yr happy alone
you tore down the world
and put up four walls
yr bleeding from every pore
yr screaming inside yr head
and you cant get me out
yr in there tonight
marshaling thoughts
you can kill the future
you can kill the past
but you cant climb out
of yr sweaty shoes
and walk away

Richard:
I never give you a thought
you've holed up
you're held up
in suspension
one too many failed tasks
one too many open roads

Musee de Ville de Paris

girl in photo by august sandler
looks across 8 decades to me
she's long dead
yet green and leafy under trees
her eyes preserved
her life force intact
what is she telling me?
to stop and linger in her gaze
to pick up on her energy
to meet her by that tree
and linger there a bit
to bang my head against her hand
and tell her we're still here.

Dust From An Old House

up late again
w blind willie
hand me my
familiar position

chairbound
strange relations
cut circles
foreign stories

pianos keyed to a chord
once upon a room

hands and faces
tacked on mirrors
look young and forward
cry further, further

down a long alley
thru an ancient screen door
the sky brightening
leaves trembling the trees

yr hand gentle
hips touching
things we never tried

i remember you now

After Winter

like, live,
you enormous lazy rock!
the only easy gift is spring
so why not fiddle a symphony in the rain
run frantic and delerious through the forest
soar out over the blue sky of eternity
think a thousand misty roads
you have yet to drive
we are all sweet summer shadows
lets not stop to sleep.

Valentine Poem

you were pushing up through the air.
you raced west, never lookin back to see what you'd left
hidden like diamonds under the wings of the world.

city gardens are
rocky reminders
in the wind the winter whispers:
thighs / lips / hair / knees

a diamond grows 10 million years of sad mist and emptiness
some would say heav'n bound, I guess.

Spanish Poet Translated 1973 by Carl High On Grass

you still could hear the overjoyous shouts. [of the sudden] I
have staid in the door looking distractedly at the going and
coming. a bird that is making its nest in the branched of an
almond tree at the point of the leaves. I remained there without
knowing why and the shades were growing y the sun had the yellow
of the juice of the ginger. Autumn was coming. A tender pain
blew shivers in me. I felt sad and I was far from what I should
be and am not. Inexpedingly I made a grimace that wanted to
disearth not needed memories. That

Every Lost Thought

This was the day of everything gone wrong. I lost all the words, mis-
placed the pictures, couldn't hear my own voice all day just a
buzzing in my head sayin *no no no that's not it that's not quite
right*. Lost lost in haste and fog. All the thoughts in my head my
whole life. All the thoughts I tried so hard and now they've all left
me.

I was witness tonight to beautiful and dangerous love, unknown and
severe; not set in any house with pictureframes on the wall although
the pictures they always end up on the wall, in wallets, all over the
place, don't they?. I remember you yr twisty tongue yr little words
dropping too fast to follow. How I hate some people but how I loved
you. All butter and pillows until ringg ring the telephone rang.

So much for history lessons.
So much for human certainties.

I was cleaning much too fast and I cleared out ev'ry lost thought in
my head.

evrything about love
evrything about money
evrything about you'nme'nher'nhim'nthem
evrything i ever wanted
evrything about pain
every feeling
evry idea
evry brick
evry instant
evry tongue
evry finger
evry memory
every one

Another Man Done Gone

I'm finished he said
almost w a sigh of relief
no more trim to scrape
no more lawns
no more wasp's nests under the eves
no more nights of TV
and empty calories
Finished he said.

To Mary

Mary
a word
a simple word
are you there
in the cold country?
mtns in yr eyes
like a tunnel?
yr mouth still full?
horses galloping
across yr pages?
i'm coming thru
doldrums thru
the trees
to wet sounds
of life. sun
filled rms.
a word just
a word
to mark yr
absence.

Train Wreck

I can't think about God
I can't see his face
can barely find this day
these road movies
But I can feel yr sigh
from here
just read yr letter
about the rain
I think about you
again and again
yr split face
yr empty shell
at the end of the cable
out on the wint'ry range
cards on the table
radiatorhissss
unbelievable nonstop conversation
Miss Understanding
you are Miss Communication
I'm an earphone
Yr. a radio tower
I love you

junkyard language
loose change
lost ideas
brand new satellites
a Mack truck *this* close
out of the woods
and onto my tongue
a blank sheet
invisible
dark skin
invisible
deep ocean
crystal spray
damp hair
the whole of you
vanishing
invisible

Notes:

Cards:
Hallowe'en
ideas
early stills
our portraits
fire-wheels
optical eye-prints
          :the name
          :the title
          :full length

Susan driving
in twenty-four frames
a walk thru woods
in single frames
on a roll
tape edits
southern exposures
rhythmic beating

notes:
from London
Moniek, so blonde
wanting the card
that cool green one
so big
and the bridge
blurred
w birds flying
west
the yellow priest
in cool
streetlampglo

Clouds

less of you
I'm thinking less of you
up under the swells
the fountain of youth
I'm too far away
and thinking less of you

code of honor
code of grace
meet me in the secret place
where i sang through you
where every good thing happened
meet me there and I'll need
less thinking of you

the streets are hidden
under wings of truth
ready to reflect
and not let up
ready to reject
time's true foul up
no step you take
can stand up
to this passing time
this hidden choice

the motel bed
soft on a rainy day
an afternoon hideout
telling some stories
finishing some things

my hands don't touch
your skin
my body moves forward
and then back

back to which day?

back to the last time
we met
when clouds were low
and our motors ran
up and down
up and down
on the street

Portland

me steve jim
and chris melfi drove
to portland today.
you wouldn't believe the
beautiful light.
sharp and hard on the trees
shaggy burnt gold grass everywhere.

did i tell you about crisp
scintillating nordic
light of Kristiansand,
Norway? *Wow.*

Murray Street

All the Chinese rain ladies
are staking sidewalk corners
chanting umbrellaumbrellaumbrella
and waititng out the storm.

Anais Nin

p. 44 House of Incest

Anais Nin
I hear this, in your voice:

"the world is too small
I get tired of playing the guitar
of knitting and walking
of bearing children
men are small and their passions short lived
I get furious at stairways
furious at doors, at walls
furious at everyday life
which interferes with the continuity of ecstasy..."

For Thom

the beautiful
sunny
afternoon
w blue sky
no clouds
it's late
and a crystalline
pristine
glow
holds the air

from this window ledge
where I sit
not even the trucks
rumbling
below me
can disturb it
the trees leave!
nice and green
the bldgs glint golden
hard edges of brick

now even
the trucks
have gone
leaving just
the hiss
of the
city

Other Images, LA 1985:

the city lit
distant
glimmering
wet
glistening
in lizard haze
of heat
and debris
struggling to
crawl along
the
constant
shifting
contour
of the earth.
unchartable.

complex freeways
passing
over
and
under.

sculptured
manicured
trees.

the desert
expanse
the night
cold
the moon
full
and
bright
with a
wild ring
thru the haze

What Lake Is Void Of Love?

for LS

you and me
two
together
luscious
languid
smooth
true
raw dream music
frantic
delicate
essential
gone elaborate girl
delirious
juice tongue goddess
bitter garden
honey nut
sweet summer peach
hot sun
gorgeous eternity

Wish Fulfilment

I see yr wishes on the wall, and that's alright with me
I see you run to make a call, hoping that there's someone free
Your life and my life they don't touch at all, and that's no way to be
You've never seemed so far...

What's real? What's true?
I ain't turnin my back on you
Where you goin? Where you been?
Making wishes, watching dreams?

It might be simple, it might be true
I might be overwhelmed by you
You might be empty—the way yr eyes just look right through

It's such a mess now anyway
Wish fulfilment every day

I don't believe you—now I can't hear a word you say

I see you shakin in the light, readin the headline news
The others aren't quite so bright, you want them to choose you
I could almost see yr face tonight, singin simple rhythm and blues
You'll always be a star...

Shake it, baby, C'mon scream
Did I see yr face in a magazine?
Your doubt, it leaves me sore
I can't stand it anymore

It's my favorite shot of you
You looked so pretty, yr eyes were true
I'm still on yr side - in spite of everything you do

We're only blood on light on life
New pretty pictures every night
Come wish beside me—don't you know you know
what's right?

New Star Light

new
star
light
quibbles
with
the
old
in
an
attempt
to
reconfigure
the
patterns
in
the
sky

Sunlight Cup

dresden, tennessee

Spill over into my hole
drag me down
a love song w no love in sight
a drained rain king
fluid slip knot
subterfuge
angry needle-guns
frozen faces
dead roads
bad smells behind closed doors
we keep it all hidden
shut from the light
the attic tomb
the cardboard museum
dust
sediment
memory
layer on layer

wasp's nest in the secret chamber
paper webbing on the beautiful wood
cobweb heroes
the lies of love

On Possessions

mere objects, should I care?
mere objects, should I care?
mere objects, should I care?
mere objects, should I care?
s;mere objects, should I care?
mere ovjects, should I caere?
m;ere objects, should I care?
mere objects, should I care?
mere objects, should I car e,
mere obmects, should I zca e.
mere objects, should I ca e.
mere obledts, shonos al care?
smere
objects
mere objects, sho ld   care?
mere oil eats, should , care
mere objects, should I care?
lmere objects, s;hould I care?
mere socvsjectan;s;hould i care/
m ere objects, s;ould I care?
mere objects, ho ld i care/
mere objects, should i care?
mere o j;ed s shou n lA care
mere id;cej
mere objectsm should i care..
;mere ;ovd enct ,should i care
;mer eo ejcjho e shouojld i aare
;mere s;objedts, shoul; d i rfe/
mere objects, should i care..
mere objects, shoulf ZI care
mere objects, should I cARW
MERE OBJECTS, SHOULD   CAR
MERE O JECTS S OULD I CARE
: MERE OBJO DSSCAREE
nere sojects, should i care?
;mere ;lovjsecrs, should i care;/?
mere objects, should i Care?
mere obects, should I care
mere objects, s o j
mere objects, sh ld i care
mere ;jb skid a;ro jhhoo o ho oyh
;m ere objects. s o ondl iu care?
j;mere; dhd;oo dldkjfdddcare?
f . . . ????
;mere jl j
mere objectsm should I care
mere objects, should I care?

In The Maelstrom Of Meaning

"the chaos of culture"
muddy
flickering
unresolved

In the maelstrom of meaning
I love more the way I feel.
I'm drawn to you
I'm spinning with you
I knock you out and then run

I love more the way I feel
when you're really real
so open to the view

I see you all over town
in little scraped together minutes
little heartbeat seconds
exposed to the light

I'm afraid of what I might do
if I might not be with you
might be empty
might be true
might be overwhelmed and unforgiven

you look so good
yr eyes not tired
yr body so well taught
I could love you all night
whisper scribbled pages
and bite you hard
the shape of my voice
the arc of my tongue
indecipherable still.

What We Did In High School

sittin around
drinkin red wine
3 in the morning
playing w/ a flashlight
in the dark

you have a talent for
writing in the dark
that's where you do
your best work.

We live in a time when imagination
is dead, you said
and everything is memories.
We call those memories *the future*.

Soon, watch
the stars will begin to multiply
and take over the sky...

Do You Read Me?

open glass
window
a new look
pointed
yellow
new sight for an old eye

movement
after
moment
time
and
again
you are picture
and sound

you are flickering now
faintly
this
signal
is weak
I'm losing
this signal
I'm

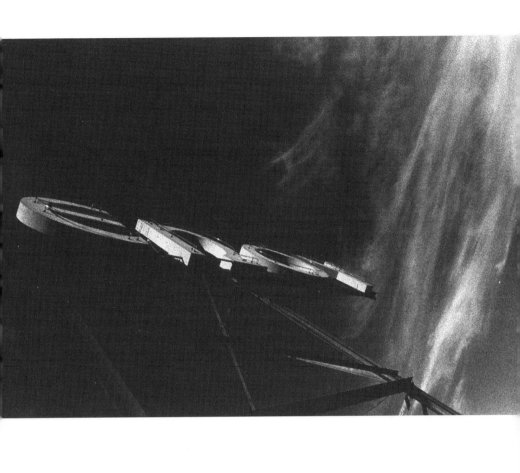

Lengths

Notebook

I stand on the balcony and wish for a cigarette as all the tiny insect lights of LA crawl back and forth below me, slithering as if on rails up into the Hollywood hills, and off into the valleys beyond them. Everyone is beautiful here, everyone has served their apprenticeship well. We live in the land of sunlight, of ripe fruit, of the fast deal and no death.

*   *   *

I watch as the whole country slides by below the wing. Deep red clays and burned out browns followed by snow-bleached peaks and now the flat geometry of the middle lands; hundreds of miles of patchwork squares and circles, an occasional bldg group here or there, isolated, and tiny city-clusters shrinking in their capillary sprawl, gray and lifeless from above.

What is this all about? The ground moving does not really alter my perspective up here. Nothing seems to affect my view these days. My life beyond stable, static. Thirty five years, ten years, almost five years, all these time line hash marks seem to have ground it to a halt. How do dreams and hopes end up frozen? How can I get back that burning desire? I'm at a standstill now. The days go in and out and I get nowhere. Still no great clang of astonishment, no brilliant flash of light, no steeple with the wide view.

All that surrounds me, all the things I have gathered and continue to gather at such an obscene rate, seem to be stones tied to the cuff, weights to make the freedom of the river that much harder to realize. And all these stupid metaphors. What is one to do? What am I to do? The idea of chukking it all seems so inviting, to throw myself headlong into a love affair, or a trip alone off in the wilds - never looking back. But I can't help myself, I always look back, life so beautiful in the rear view, everything in golden light and very still. Faces, places, feelings, thoughts, embalmed forever:

That wall in Chapel Hill.
Karen lying on the bed, by that sunshaded window, Johnson City, listening for footsteps and not yet through.
The soft mountains, green, at seven years old, and eight, and nine.
Lori's face in that photograph.
The old Volkswagen, parked by the gate of those brown fields, that red tractor leaving traces as it plodded across before Thom and I, our eyes wild with it.
La Sagrada Famiglia in Barcelona.

Los Angeles' palm trees looming like endless flagpoles, and reflected
overhead in all the rear windows like arching spiders.
Hovering just twenty minutes ago above the cotton ball clouds.
The first gig in Berlin.
Mudd Club with the gate coming down.
The stained glass windows of St. Dom's seen close up, the movie
camera view.
All the envelopes full of tiny snapshots, collecting dust.
My mother as a small girl in a burnished white dress.
My wife as a young mother.
All the girls whose initials have been L.S.
The feeling of almost drowning beneath the placid blue surface.
Kissing Mary in the dark.
Old movies, my first attempts, all hazy and bleached out blue.
Cody in his leather jacket.
Amanda driving the old wrecked blue Plymouth across the Canadian
landscape.

My life in a frozen moment, a fly's eye faceted view of all the
moments which make up the full strand. Do any of these moments
mean even the slightest thing? Michael dragging off the opium pipe
in the shaded green of his backyard. How much easier if the past
were a black hole, if we had amnesia.

Bright sun skating its way in fractured kite-like beads through the
pine trees outside Susan's house: how many of my memories are
created, or reinforced, by the documentation of them? Do we film
events only to be able to see them in retrospect, to see them as
though they were the actual moments themselves burned onto our
retinas? To see them as though they were really what we saw at the
time, instead of just what we imagined them to be? I don't remem-
ber anything. I only recall pictures. Snapshots of events I may have
been present at. Televised pictures of the revolution, nowhere near
here, are mine, too. I recall written words of my own past equally
with those of times and places I have little business knowing any-
thing about. I've never really been to sea. Never driven down an
endless straight ribbon of highway into the next state. Never floated
on a Swiss alpine lake, or burrowed deep into the earth's fossil corri-
dor of time.

Is it even possible to reach out and touch another person? To dent
their flesh with my fingertips? Why all the conventions, the walls to
prevent such happenings? What can you show me?? What can I tell
you? How many years have we been apart? Where have you been all
my life? When can I see you again? I'm sick of the sight of you. All
the dichots head-butting one against the other, tearing my soul in
two directions at once, ripping at the seams of my consciousness.
Babbling on and on in my mind.

NYC Ghosts And Flowers

for NMR, CLR & SLR

when the phone rang, 3 in the morning, dead middle of night
there was nuthin on the line
i set back the silent receiver / tiny flames lit in my head
hey did any of you freaks here ever remember lenny?
i can't remember his last name...
he's turned to dust now, one of the chosen few
left out in the rain, out of town again...
left out in the rain, ocean bound i guess...

between the mattress and a column of hazy faces
i remember every word you said
quite a clear picture: ev'ry word you said
the door was open but the way was not lit
and there was no way out of my head...

on a crimson hiway by a chrome bumper i last saw you:
alive / inclined to thrive / evening fireflies lit sparks around yr head

           *   *   *

now here at dark corners all is calm and quiet and good
the kids are up late dreaming quiet questions in a graceful mood:

      can you please pass me a jug of winter light?
      fold me in an ocean's whim?
      in sweet corrosive fire light?
      in the city made of tin?

      are you famous under the skin?
      familiar with the things you wanted?
      able now to take it all in?
      making peace w every hole in the story?

      did lightning keep you up all night?
      illuminate the soot and grit?
      can you tell how high the sky tonight?
      dig out from under in spite of it?

      can you cover up the one that floats?
      can you push back the hours?
      i hear yr voice, i speak yr name
      among nyc ghosts and flowers
      will we meet? to run again?
      thru nyc ghosts and flowers...

I'm In Between Times
And Tired Of This Wait

254 years
an endless love
yr dark hair
what happened?

N. Carolina
Hemingway
Topless Bars
Ghetto Blasters
Planet Waves
all you want.

I'm talking
1963
THE
BIRTH
OF
TIME

my sister
couldn't be here
my childhood
ended w the rain
the river rising

S Wash St
steel bridge
over the river
riding high
over the
rushing water

put it all behind me
now it's all behind me

bombarded by sound
loved ones neglected
while PA's scream
for my attention

I can't hear you
These times don't add up.
I can't reach you

These times don't add up.

Don't ask another question
about ten years ago.
Put away the concerns
that kept you up late.
Say so long to the years
that died behind you.
Goodbye to everyone
that held in the fear.

little pricks on the phone
I was one, remember?
the image of abandon
the tunnel of love
rhythm of the tracks
the sound of a bell

Yr jigsaw image,
now that's the whole of you.
Yr skin and yr hair
rock the street.
The shotgun floor
cushions my head.
I see it
I felt it
I was at that door

Here it is October.
I haven't been home
in six months.
Goodbyes have all been said,
packed up in trunks.
Dead seasons jam
all the gears.
The whole thing
has been unloaded.

Bloomington, Indiana: Autumn

I cannot concentrate
Everything before me blurrs together
until nothing is sharp, or simple
Our lives mixed up, and complicated
In the bookstore I can barely see
to let a few words from some page through

All these words collide
and jostle one another: Anne Sexton:
I open at random and find 'Sylvia's Death'
which then
bumps against biographical blurbs on Dylan, and Joni,
A children's book about weasels
and how life consumes life
A map of the heavens, every star illuminated
A recollection of some long lost memory

The courthouse square, my head still for a moment
The breeze scattering jewel-like leaves all at my feet
Burnt violet, bright yellow, mottled reds and oranges
I press a few into my book, why?
Have you kicked through leaves, in the city?
Let them come up under your toe?
Well I have, out here, while thinking of you.

I cannot concentrate, cannot shut off this day
How I'd love to do it clear.
Where am I, amidst these blowing leaves
which shake shake shake and fall
through the telephone wires?

The world is too full,
I wait for it to spill at my feet
like these leaves
Your eyes appear everywhere:
in the green lawns,
and upon these frozen statues
The jade plants in this window echo your stage name
I am late and I do not care
Absent from where I should be
Neglectful of my duties
Trying to sort out these various avenues
which run to and fro

I have made a new book from all the random pages

The story the same no matter how we sequence it
Change is in the heart
The head waits, and follows, a slower creature
and that is what I am doing, now

Waiting
for this pursuit to end
Waiting
to see you again
You or anyone who can disconnect me
Show me some new language
Close the car door
Find the nearest exit.

Help me clear this up
Help me keep this feeling
Help me save these thoughts,
which I want to hold so much
Help me see this through.

LA—>NYC

Another moment, another air-bound memo.   Another plane in vain.
Not a single idea clear and held by its stem. No words that are not free
floating. Let me grab a thought from the air. Help! Can't put two and
two together.   Can't turn an inference into a surety.   Happiness is
healthiness. What is wildness?

Wilderness is far flung and far from me. No invented stories. No white
water. I don't believe in fiction. I don't believe anyone has much to
say that will make a difference. I don't believe the movie is starting.
don't believe in indulging whims, only fantasies. Fantasies great and
small.

I believe in writing in the dark, in small change and the printing press.
In pretty girls and the hard highway. The road is round. The sky is an
envelope. The woods may be green but I'm not there. Kids may rock
and roll and get rowdy as hell but I'm no longer there. I've done those
things. Some things. I need to shut the window and find a new
metaphor. Stand in the midst of a grand idea and hold fast. How many
can say they've found a new one? Only the chosen few. The new cow-
boys who ride between the thought clouds, across the tables of knowl-
edge. Frozen in place, splattered across the landscape.

Where are the lists of our beliefs? Crazy jumbles of images, wild layers of sound, words tumbling out one on the next — these are the shapes and manifestations of today. Everyone knows that overlaid images are the true reality — the levels of meaning exposed, only to blurr together in a new formation, unreadable, inseparable one from the next.

But I want to see clearly, that one image, and slow it down, incredibly slow so as to frame by frame life, examine it in minute detail. The two minutes that take ten years (or more) to live out. Yes let's do that. Stretch one hour of life over twenty, Let three minutes equal one hour (not the reverse! not now!). Stretch time out like a concise book serial or that episode of The Outer Limits where the clocks ran slow as the truck beats down on the little girl on her bike in the street, one man walking amidst the slow moving vehicles the way we walk among the rocks, among alabaster statues. Hold on to description, hold on to language. Let the ideas roll forth. Let the lights twinkle and burn across the night. Then stop dead as one idea ceases and none rise up to follow.

The light within me shines, like a diamond mine, like an unarmed walrus, like a dead man face down on a highway, like a snake eating its' own tail, a steam turbine, frog pond, too-full closet burst open in disarray, soap bubbles in the sun, hospital death bed, red convertible, shopping list, blow job, death's head, devils dancing, bleached white buildings, memory movements; the movie, unreeling, about to begin.

Dirty Windows

Pelts! Human pelts for sale - get 'em while they still stink.   On Seventh Avenue by West Fourth Street a Puerto Rican girl is scream- ing at a black guy, they're pushed up very close. Jade and I are walking by, night. I wasn't making out with him! she screams. Bitch! Bitch! he's yelling back. Then as we're moving along: I didn't stick my tongue in his mouth! O yeah you bitch! Amazing how quickly this arguement escalated from one thing to the next. I wanted to turn to look but only did at the last moment as we rounded some construc- tion, fearing she'd point me out to him and he'd come at me with his six inch gold blade next. This film tonight was full of brutal stab- bings, and I don't like knives one bit, having once been on the hold- ing end, staring at the gash.

Let me take you to the last scene first and work backwards across this thing: this gripping film, as they say - this is the picture the term was made for - which took all of about two and a half minutes, seemingly, to inject it's tale into my skull. Or was it up my ass, jam- ming in another nail, maybe?

Last shot* : the white hero cop laying in the dirt outside the old house as his backups pull up, his multiple wounds filling with dust, his flannel shirt a bloody wreck. He's cradling a little black boy - his unknowing son - in his arms. The boy's mom is shot on the porch, a hole in her forehead, alongside her scheming companions. The pros from LA are too late. He's laying, dying, holding this little boy cra- dled in his arm. Her brother could've saved her, but he chose to hide her out, and helped to kill her. The cop himself could've owned up to having fucked her and fathered this little child, too, but he also helped kill her instead. After all he had an eight year old of his own at home, with a white woman, of course. The dick from LA was slip- ping whiskey into his morning coffee, he too a lost fuck up. The rest were all hicks, hoodlums or slow. They all died in the end. When it's finally revealed that this bumpkin cop who's going to try to be the hero had fucked the beautiful black girl and fathered her child, it was all just too clean and pretty. So why should the end of this movie have been so affecting? Why did we walk home in silence, one full hour, all these filthy visions of this city drifting by, all these contra- dictions playing out before our eyes? I can't even recount them all now in any fair sequence, but thoughts seemed to unfold like a true short story - which is what this movie was, and why we like short sto- ries - not just Carver's either - and why movies approximate them, in one sitting.

I spoke to Cody on the phone today - this is the first thing I thought, thinking about that little boy in the movie - Daddy are you gonna see

---

* *One False Move,* Carl Franklin, dir.1992

me today? That's the kind of question kids ask these days. Yeah I'm
gonna see you, son. Can we baseball, baseball, baseball? Yeah,
guess we can. I spent the day trying to sell some records. Talking
about myself. Feeding some bland new images to the world.

When a bum brushed Jade's shoulder and spazzed off some fat girls
in suburban clothes standing on the corner with their boyfriends
laughed like the idiots they were. Signs everywhere are advertising
every little last lame thing, and in these dark streets after all those
blades every person seems treacherous, an enemy, especially on the
darkest streets. Under the flourescence of a Citibank sign a black
man lay with his shirt off on the sooty marble, only his eyes which
followed us giving any sign of life.

In Koln, Germany a few nights back, on a small street I walked along-
side a polished XJ6 with it's engine running, parked in the darkened
lane, and it was only after a moment that I realized the driver was
getting head from a local street walker. Gay men were walking arm
in arm, in relative peace under the dark quiet night there.

The tape plays music made on insturments fashinoned exclusively
from human remains; skulls and bones echoing in a subteranean
cave...

On a night like this I fear for the lives of my loved ones, and discount
all dreams. Here I walk beside this beautiful young woman, she's
finishing her chocalate ice cream. But another love sits home,
alone, tonight, are they pushing in her screen window at this very
moment?

Fuck the icons and media salesmen. Fuck the baseball players and
the president. Fuck Marilyn Monroe, up there too in a window, she
died 30 years ago and I don't have any designs on her corpse. How
unimportant she is, really. What else, what else? Human pelts, get
em now! All words escape me now. All pictures of this silent night.
I've written a book in my head, oh yeah, and fuck me too, most of
all, because you'll never read it.

The carnival machines were all folded up and the lights in the
square were being taken down further up Seventh Avenue. The
streets were filled with people, beautiful ones in tight black, and
ugly ones in flapping bolts of frayed and faded cloth, and they each
had a movie flashing in their heads, all playing out at once. I can't
hear any of them right now. Why do they all seem to be suffering,
nearly laying down in these dirt awful streets?

On Fifth Avenue above Fourteenth Street some people behind us
were yelling and we crossed the street, avoiding the shadows under
the trees. All the shop windows dead, waiting to scream into the

traffic again, come daylight.

Jade, yr bare foot goes up and down beside me now, and I'm excep-
tionally comforted knowing it's you here, yet I wonder if I'll ever be
free to enjoy this moment, with yr lovely tapping foot; free of all the
ghosts and real people crowding around me.

My mother called and I happened to pick up the phone at Duane
Street. Well well do you recognize my voice? I guess you just
haven't had time for thinking of us, have you? It's been three weeks!
I guess we just don't rate anymore. I'd been away, true, but now
home three days I could only stammer and wonder where all the time
goes. Been busy...

I've got projects, Projects, do you hear? Left right and center, above
and all around me now, not least of which is baseball bsball bsball
with Cody, and every second of these days now is being consumed
with endless activity. Some people should be so lucky...

swing leg, swing
draw me into a world of the flesh
draw me closer to ev'ry spinning image
lead me on into rosy sunlight
grass
green
love
life
drumming
drumming
scratching at all these
dirty windows
knocking
hard
on
all the panes
one ending
following another
crescendo upon crescendo
wave
wave
wave
never letting up
never letting up
pounding the message home.

Time Presses Me

(some kind of time line)

1953 RE-ENTRY
1954
1955
1956 TIME BEGINS (AGAIN)
1957 THE WORLD
1958 THE DAY
1959 HISTORY REPEATS ITSELF
1960 DAWN OF TIME
1961
1962 THE VOID
1963 MEMORY
1964 EMPTY ORBIT
1965
1966 THE PARADE ROUTE
1967 CANDLES
1968
1969 THE SACREMENTS
1970
1971
1972 STARLIGHT SHIFT
1973 THE JOY OF A PARKED CAR
1974 THE TIDE IS HIGH
1975
1976 WE REACH THE TREES
1977
1978 CORNBALL REALISM
1979 ROUND SOUNDS
1980 NEW DECISION
1981 EMPTY HEADED VESSEL
1982 THE ABYSS
1983 HEALING HANDS
1984
1985 TIME PRESSES ME
1986 I SANG THRU YOU
1987
1988 THE MULTITUDE
1989
1990 THIS INFINITE SEASON
1991
1992 SLOW REPEAT
1993
1994 WAVE LENGTH
1995 QUASI OPUS
1996
1997 THE GREEN SCENE
1998
1999 SHIFT

Cedar Bar

at night we fight
and furiously
but then something goes awry
and we're talking again
by morning somewhere
hatred dissolved
somehow I'm in love with you again

I'm not sure why this is
but a hatred of this life
easily translates
to hating you
the slap of flesh
alleviates the pain
this need to strike out
and protest
every thing
that has not come my way
ev'ry drug-addled night
ev'ry sea-sick morning
ev'ry yearning desire
that knocked me off course
that set me adrift

I'd rather be kissing you now
it's true
hold you tight and
never let go
but this feeling returns
again and again
each time the night comes closing in
and I'm fed up with everything
bored in this hated house

when we're not fucking
or talking
or out with friends
or otherwise escaping
from these ordinary days
that open one into the next,
let's confess to aging sunlight
and graying walls
and losing that steadfast grip
on life eternal

let's confess to no longer
being anywhere near as
young as the faces of
the children in the
pictures we bring home
from the fotomat

might as well hand off now
to our children and their friends
as they look out from the frame
still young,
still innocently gazing
still unaware of the roadblocks to come
still in awe of life ahead.

Skip Tracer

This she did in public, for us to see:
She came in here to be too drunk to do the show
Between the trains and cars, broken glass and lost hubcaps:
Images of a gun

Row house row house pass thru, let the city rise up to fill the screen
Clothes flung outta closets / Doorknobs falling off

The gtr guy played real good feedback, and super sounding riffs
He had his mild mannered look on—man, he was truly hip
The girl started in red patent leather, very "I'm-in-a-band", with
kneepads
We watched her fall over and lay down
Shouting the poetic truths of high school journal keepers

Row house row house pass thru, let the city rise up
Twister, dust buster, hospital bed, I'll see you see you see you on the
hiway
Now we tone-soul merge ideas of song forms and freedom
Miss Seafood, Miss Cheesecake, a coupla Miss Donuts
The edge of the blade pressed to the throat of yr reflected image
Poised, yet totally skrewed up
Yes sir yes sir step right up

None of us know / where we're tryin ta get to
What sort of life? What we're tryin ta build

Now we tone-soul merge ideas, of song forms, and freedom
Seasons out of life / nothing is out of reach
LA is more confusing,now, than anywhere I've ever been to
I'm from New York City, breath it out and let it in
Where are you now, when yr broken eyes are closed?
Head in a cloudy dream of green and sailboats?
Borrowed and never returned, emotions, books, outlooks on life...

Hello 2015!!

Deva, Spain

Some people are walking slow out of the rolling, slowly ramping
Spanish sea. It's 2:30 AM, there's not much light, very little moon
but many stars and an occasional pair of headlights running fences
along the coastal road, rounding the bends, swinging in and out of
view. A man lies on the beach. From this balcony he's nothing more
that a tiny white blip on all this dark - with the sandy beach a faint
curve on the shore. Another tiny light, a woman, is just stepping
from the water's edge onto the sand, heading for him. There is a
second couple in the water, taking their time, heading in. The gentle
incline of the sea allows that they are quite far out, yet still the
water is not deep. The surf is breaking in long white extended rib-
bons, rolling slowly away from us down the beach.

There is no light, no white only greys and black, a deep charcoal
drawing. Pinpoint stars. We zoom in and the couple in the water fill
the frame. Her eyes close, the two of them near but not touching,
him gesturing. What are they saying? They're trying to be reason-
able. They love each other: this much is clear. How to balance the
tides which surround them?

Then it is her pressing him: *I can't go on like this* and *What shall
become of us?* He echoes back, *Yes, yes, I feel the same* and reaches
to touch her, running his hand across her shoulder and up the nape of
her neck. They stop to look at each other, silent but for the sea. We
keep the sound of the rolling surf but cut to the other two in a medi-
um shot, laying on the smooth, dark sand. They're far enough away
from our water couple that theirs is a private conversation. These
two on the beach have no vested interest in this. Just distant watch-
ers.

They talk on, the two in the water. They walk down the edge of the tide, ankles still in. He's smoking now, and she looks at him. They're speaking in low tones. They talk seriously, then veer off onto some tangent which captures them both for a moment, cars still winding around the dark turns. Their laughter is carried by the breeze along the length of the dark beach. We can see that she pushes against him playfully before they pull back, and turn serious again. Love is pulling them together, and pushing them apart.

We are two funny little magnets, she says, smiling at him, her eyes full.

We are it, he says, and *this is what's real, now.*

Later, in the barren hotel room, five flights up, they are laying together, the balcony door open to the sea and the first of the morning sun. The room holds a large bed, a small plain wooden desk. Two travel bags sit in a corner. There is a movie camera lying nearby on the floor as well, but little else. The room itself is a half circle, with the bed against the diametric wall, the curved wall full of tall thin windows, a ring of them, with sheer curtains filtering the early sun, and wooden shutters in various states of repair. In some the cords have broken, leaving certain windows permanently dark, and others forever half-open.

Not all the shutters work, she had told him. *Not all of them go all the way up.*

They talk about silly things this morning, before coffee or anything else. They lie naked together under a thin sheet, soft light filtering in through the curtains. This is an easy day; they momentarily escape together. They laugh and tell each other new things, old things. They tell each other some things they can tell no-one else. We hear the sea. The room is smooth, with cream-colored walls, the door frame and sills a deep yellow. The sea is blue. The hills are lush and green. Some children on the beach are shouting, swimming already at this early hour, and kicking a ball through the sand. A black dog is splashing around the shoreline, waiting for them.

They know that this idle must soon end. Together or apart, that is what they are wondering. They sit on the sea-terrace with coffee from the bar. Later they walk the alleyways of the old town, make love in the room at midday, and again as the sun is setting. They lie in the still-warm sand, late in the afternoon when the crowds have gone. They move in and out of their situation, bound and weighed by time, and decisions to be made.

I love you. It is you for me now, he says. This is for you.

Everything is for you, now. This thought is for you. You are in my head, now; in my present tense. This will not go away before we see it through. The edge of life is near and I feel at this moment ready to jump across it.

Wedding Day Pome

Leah Singer

I wish you would sit here.
Clear a place amidst this debris
I want to tell you how
I expect to see you walking a wire
between the sea and the shore

When the lights change we'll both jump
I'll read yr name in books and see yr smile on the evening news
We shall be great friends, tell each other great thoughts
and hear great sounds together.

We analyze sensations. We venture a caress.
We imagine the cinema yet live in the real world.
The cinema is dreams, memories, things I've read, and YOU.
You are a stretch of beautiful frames,
unwinding from the spool each time we meet.

I have crawled inside yr life. And you mine.
In the afternoon it poured rain.
Thunder and flash lightning.
I couldn't stop thinking of you.
Thought maker
Picture-taker
Everything in the room is abstract
except the sound of yr voice
the curve of yr body

You inform my days
in subtle ways;
as I walk down the street
or sit chair-rooted,
thinking Technicolor.

You are reflected
walking innocent like a saint

pitching a fight against boredom
in row boat dreams
green w Canada geese
and four-leaf children.
Eyes flecked with certainty
glazed with visions
laughing at questions
holding out answers

The sun is silent
The air is brilliant
My eyes are open
My ears are ringing still
w the sound of you

You and I share EcStaSY
Not the endless rhythm of monotonous days
but the sparks that can fly

I wrote your name in the snow, three times
the last coupled with my own.

Free At Last

january

free at last, free at last, thank god almighty, free at last, to lay back
and forget about the proper rules of etiquette.....to be a perfect
slob and feel at home with the truth. chicago tonight is a cold place
in a cold world. i feel the polar night coming on...

dear T,

hi, hello, how are you? i'm in chicago now and sitting in the late
afternoon darkening living room to write you. eighty-seven is here
and i'm looking forward to a good good year. these last few weeks
of xmas-time have been somewhat of a hell for the most part. I've
not felt much in the way of spirit this year, and the scenes at both of
our family houses have been less than i'd've liked them to be. that's
too bad, too, because as i walk these cold streets here in chicago or
downtown oyster bay i know that there is a peaceful feeling to be
had that's impossible in nyc where everyone is rushing around in a
hurry.

i must say that the two nights you and jeff and i managed to steal
away were without a doubt the high points—an affair long forgotten
and sorely missed, i hadn't felt such close and needed TALK in a long
time, even if we werent always talking specifically about "some-
thing". That wasn't the point, which was, rather, that we COULD
talk—about ANYTHING, said anything to each other and found solace
and insight there from each other. as i may have said that night, i
feel that we are all entering a new stage now, having come from the
times we used to talk when the future was wide for all of us, through
the times when we each gradually went our own ways to find our
lives. now, anyway, we're all in a new place again, similar amongst
ourselves in our plights. we're all SOMEWHERE now, and it's time to
look up and evaluate exactly where the hell that is. i know that for
myself it's meant the revival of much questioning that i hadnt had
time for in these last few years of "getting there", but now i see
that things must change for me and it's time to reopen the file, to
begin asking questions now, because if not now then i'll one day
wake up and it'll all be over, i'll not have noticed the time flying by.
and let's face it, it goes all too fast as it is without it's going unrec-
ognized to boot.

anyway, tomorrow we leave chicago and return, hopefully, to a few
months of peace and industrious work. i'm reading yet another biog-
raphy of old jacky, called 'desolate angel', and it's the very best one
i've come across so far. so once again my head is filled with those
folks and their times, their visions and hopes.

hope all is well. it's been a long time since i wrote you a real bona-
fide lettre, hasn't it?

w love

Santa Monica

everything is strange here
as if in dream
i creep silent in the sun
not thinking of yr voice
i slip thru nighttime conversations
wondering what to say
listening to yr voice on the phone
drive wide green streets

LA is all green
I am uprooted
everyone rushing into the light
everyone hoping to win
I GOT MINE! I GOT MINE!!

If I stand fast, I shall be a slave
dipping deeper down
peeking thru the branches
the world hot and dry
that dusty blue carpet
where your feet were lightly walking
is matted down

every face from the past
is talking at once
in a bar
on the sidewalk
on a side street
in postcards and on
the telephone
they're all dressed kinda funny
hands flopping around
i can't see how
they all fit in
where they/ve come from
or where they go
they vanish in thin air
still talking nonsense
still looking for a scheme
to hang life on
still waiting for a vision to love
a reason to be

saying over and over

tired
drooping
to one person
after the next
"No, I'm not hungry, thanks."
I'm just tired and in need of sleep
in need of some new religion
a new set of clothes
and a new idea to cart away
all the old things
not shiny but new
calm and clear
no veil of fuzz

This Is The Way We Wash The Car

this is the way...
THE QUICK BROWN FOX JUMPS OVER THE LAZY DOG.
the quick brown fox jumps over the lazy dog.,./;'[,.?:"]::,;;:::::
th thick bromm   c
    hi hi hi hi hi hi hi hi hi   l
hjh

leah is a lazy bone!

LEAH IS A LAZYBONE!
leah izza lazybones!
LEAHBONES!
LEAH, BONED!
lee boned leah
LEEBONED!
LEAHLAZZYBOWED!
LIZABO
LEAHBO '
LEAHBOL
LEAHBONES
LOOPY HEADED FEVER JOINTS
TRAGI COMIC SWAMP CITY
TRAGIC CEREAL BOX
TRAGIC MATCHES
SILLY PUTTY HAND JOB
SATANIC CRANKSHAFT HOLY HEAD
HOLY HOLY HOLY LORD GOD OF HOSTS

HEAVEN AND EARTH ARE FILLED WITH YR MOTEL ROOMS,
SAUNABATHS, CLOUD CHAMBERS, DREAM THEORIES, SINGLE BULLET
CONVICTIONS:

APRON STRINGS UNTIED,LANOLIN SKIN-FLAKES,TORN CURTAINS,
REAR WINDOW GAZERS, JUICY LADYBOXES,LETHAL LAZYBONES,
LADYBUG EARRINGS,

This is the way we wash the car...

holy holy holy lorg god of hosts
heaven and earth are filled with yr motel rooms,
filled with yr hot boxes lonely ladies lost children
ancient ruins, train ticket stubs. tired watches,
dried martinis, shattered eyeglasses, burnt offerings
paper scraps next to lost hubcaps

i can see between yr eyes of blue
and read between the lines of you

I Thought Of You, Sadly

for MG

i'm not in love with love. new york city tonite and the whole thing is
brought so much closer to home. the whole picture in a less-fuzzy
frame. cruising 4 a.m. streets not knowing if i recognize this place or
what. all the people in the club, they're new york but not the new
york i knew, i guess that's gone already. which is real? this city with
all this action and faces and words-thoughts-feelings? or this quiet
fence around my head, drawing tighter each year?

kissing mary in the club, all that skin... keep away mary, there is no
need-to-burn here.

all this city, all these thoughts to grab hold of. why does cruising the
NJ turnpike before dawn, all the lights glistening, seem somehow
more real than friends and faces in front of me? does it hold more of
that great emptiness that really is the world to see an empty high-
way?

all the mail, all the letters lost, and a voice says "i thought of you,
sadly." what an epic thought there. all the straight talk in the world
can't quench my thirst, or pull at this deep tone. the abyss, the
crack in the world. i begin to slip through tonite. is this the dream?

this ringing sensation behind my eyes? is it a passing myth?

"athens, her columns white like bones against the blue...".

what is the thought that slipped away? all these stupid bldgs trying
for a din to quench all thought. that blonde girl laughing and trying
to come on. no hope in sight.

"i thought of you, sadly." you were part of my landscape. once i
walked across yr back but now your memory in my head holds up a
good part of the world, skies that have passed over me, ticking off
years.

i slipped across yr belly
and landed on yr mouth
the instant thrill of you
some kind of NOW moves between us
like a river nearing its end
there's a time held somewhere just for us
if things go on long enough
so hard and hot/so sweet and wet

this theoretical affair we have
ramming you home in thin air
all the lonely eyes are watching. a world behind eyelids is turning on
and off. in a crowded bar all the images swirl and mix and when it
empties out so does all the hope. all the hopes stand staring at wish-
ing their kiss on our lips.

eyes melt, glazed, unpolished, futile.
you love me a minute,
we can almost see clear to the end,
my face in yr hair, mine alone then.

legs
lips
neck
hair
all that skin

you got a hard on
i dont need one
you say yr no fun
i got a shotgun

everybody's building themselves an ocean
everybody's got their own little boat
they plan on leaving later this winter
heading away from the coast.

A Bit Of Memory

summer's almost on
the diamond days ahead
i can feel it
the need to immerse
to pull under its' cover
its' foggy haze

i can take it all in
and open the gate
throw sand in the cracks
and watch it filter down

this is the end of the day
these are the times of our lives
talking, hoping
laying in wait
trying to stumble across something sensible

all the boys tighten their belts and
stick it to each other
who is on top?
who is in place?

open the papers
and tell me the news
light up the pages
WAIT for tomorrow
climb down off that truck...

Ignition:
charged up
screaming in the din
waiting for nothing
I remember every word you said
each time we meet
I can't remember yesterday
but I can remember
ten years ago
when nothing was important
and everything mattered
QUITE A CLEAR PICTURE
the back porch was so significant then
gleaming glasses on sunlit tables
green and gold and brown...
you said nothing was important
and everything mattered

epic discussions and then
I'd meet you in the bedroom
sliding across your body
late in the night
while they're talking next door
through thin walls
under low lights
meeting in the bedroom
and not speaking a word

a dead end world
of memory floods
ideas under water
wet as stones
all the machinery rusted
till nothing was left
our house itself raised
I set up a room on yr porch
it was summer by then
the cats slept in the middle of the driveway
the light shot straight through the pines
from Syracuse all the way to Binghamton

a room for me on yr porch
you danced around me in that room
the last time I really had friends
was the last time I really had none
a group without enmity, ended
they tore the house down
and tarred it over...

Memory is an epic poem, an endless story, the details shifting in place. Hazy light on dim faces, photos turning grey. I need a fulcrum to lift each day now, to elevate need to a burning desire. I remember the pressing need, the longing, the beautiful empty feeling of wanting, of being incomplete. But that was long ago. I can't remember how it went. Now nothing matters, and everything, every damned thing, is important. Memories are forever backing up, mixing up, jumbled and unclear. All that i have left to strive for, each event these days, means less and less. And yet every damn thing is so important.

Certainly The Lack Of Stars Overhead Serves To Suppress Certain (Essential) Thoughts In City Dwellers

Here's a package of stuff—
a token from the arc of my desire:

> Obscure clouds
> Genius lore
> Medication
> Slo movies
> Lost angles
> Third reasons
> Empathy
> Miss Go-Lightly
> Crooked telephone poles
> Laughing hysterically
> (head banging against the locker)
> Beyond fluid thought

Dear J:

Hello from somewhere out in america. Do you know how great it was getting yr letter before i left (just before/..)? I want to write you back for real, and will (and know you won't hold yr breath) but its been very hard these days to think even one clear thought. I'm in the middle of some things, and waiting for the dust to clear a bit. I'm really feeling quite a long ways out... Was good to hear from you— things sound good! I can't wait to see you in california. Hope yr (all) well—my address is always good— XXX

*   *   *

The bell has just rung on the first race of the day. The present tense is a near-impossible thing to accomplish. Spending that whirling week together under the lights in Reno—shitty hotel rooms—sleeping in the car—argument at Zabriski Point—all of it— helped to set me straight. Now, for this minute, I am sure these things really happen; now i am sure of it.

*   *   *

Those tree-shadows in the park here, all whispering,
shish-ing leaves, around 6 PM, shadows across the cob-
blestones—

Sound here: rain, distant thunder and car horns, traffic
sounds far off

The couple enter a movie theatre, shots of them
descending the escalator into the theatre lobby and
examining the posters, the candy stand. They sneak in
when the attendant is called away for a moment. We
see them file down the left hand aisle and lean against
the wall. The film has begun some time before. They
are observing the audience in their seats instead of the
film on the screen. We listen to them talk as though
oblivious to their surroundings—she relates a story to
him of something she overheard that morning, something
she saw transpire in the park. He takes out a flash cam-
era and snaps one of the crowd, who erupt in protest
and annoyance. He apologises, claims an accident. A
moment later he triggers the flash again, and the audi-
ence becomes angry, shouting, at the two of them.
She's giggling into his collar. The attendant is coming
down the aisle, they beat a hasty retreat, up the escala-
tor and running into the street, look both ways and
jaunt off in wet streets.

We examine the stills he took, one after the other, at
faces upturned, absorbed in the lights reflecting off the
screen.

                *   *   *

She's standing on the street near a wall and a guy comes
running up, disheveled and hastily shouting, followed by
another, each holding a can full of house paint. She's
caught between them arguing or rehearsing a scene or
something. They revolve around her, their bantering
never stops, they don't see her at all. She spins in a
circle, watching and listening, spellbound and per-
plexed. Each man screams a final point, flinging the
cans of paint high up at the wall, one after the other.
Two colors smear and run. Her coat now flecked with
color, she's left there on the street bewildered and cast-
ing about after they run off. People walking by glance
from her to the dripping wall and back again.

                *   *   *

Sparks and manic blasts push with velocity against
the stone canyons downtown. Echoes of shots seem
to come from everywhere, w no apparent source of
origin. We are in the mine field; we are in the mind
field. Not one of us will lose our way. I promise. I'll
hold yr. Hand. I'll shield your eyes from the glare.

We saw:
    Continents fading
    How the elevator goes up
    The sound kettle
    Mirrored rooms
    The first images of man, in stone
    Constellations
    Hydro-carbon chains
    The infinite scale of atomic time
    Thomas Edison, in palms
    The Groove
    Colour spectra
    Weightlessness
    3 D TV
    Giant eye balls and spinning psychodiscs
    A brief glimpse of god
    Towers to the sun

    Solid blue sky
    w mixed and brushy
    grounds.
    A surge of land
    Horizons muted like Rothko's chapel
    blue w white and pink
    blacks, ochres, indian red, indigo, sienna
    yellow-green, ultramarine blue, prussian deep.

    The landscape of a country
    The landscape of an apartment
    The landscape of a body and a face
    The tabletop landscape of a conversation
    The landscape of the bedroom

Dear C:

Out w Neil, as you may have heard. It's pretty cool, mostly. My life is a whirlwind these days, I'm tring to pull various thoughts from the thin air. How are you doing?

The Kid

In his head, the Kid slowly cycles towards half-speed, adjusting to the boredom of normalcy; a madman tone-ing down, sighting through shades of grey where once he saw psychedelic colors...

When had the change come? With familiarity, mainly. Hipped to the language. How true the world. He sees nothing at first, can barely see himself. Slowly actions happen around him and to him, his blinders begin to erode. His picture starts to paint. He moves into a bigger world.

He gets more and more caught up, his life becomes bold and rich. Yet he finds himself growing unsure, less able to see himself as clearly as he did when he was all there was to see. The earth trembles beneath him. the erosion of his self, he begins to go under. He makes love to the drug, his old visions recede into the past. He can't tell if they ever really existed at all. He looks and thinks.

"I can't keep control of my thoughts. Did I really ever think like that? Are those my thoughts I'm thinking? If my mind was a file cabinet," he thinks, "I could pull the file on those thoughts, and check it out, in front of me."

All he can do is think, try to think: what is the present? When was the past? What was it that happened there? Where are we now? Do we dream? The Kid stands mute trying to look down the street and he imagines he's looking down the knife-like edge of the world. Cutting away the crap. He tries and he fails.

Now he's a shell, caught up in the facts of his breakfast table. His ride to work. His conversations. He smiles and says: "We're all working towards the same thing."

He tries to tow the day to day images along, to place them end to end and see the continuity. The year to year cartography. Once he couldn't love, now he can love and can also lose because of it, never knowing if love is on or off, yes or no, if he's in ecstasy or near death. "I see you in a different light each morning," he tells his wife, "how can i ever know you? You're not me, I'm not even me most of the time."

He looks down at his hands and then away, through the room to the window. Outside a cloud is slowly stretching, unfurling, between two very tall buildings. There is a beautiful deep quality to the blue of the sky. Has he ever seen it like that before? "Christ I don't even know!" he cries almost aloud. "I can't hold the image! I can never be sure!"

He breaks down into some kind of mumbling Ur-language murmur. Almost talking to himself, but not quite, not yet. He can't make it back to level one, not at this point. He tries for a long time to finally comprehend this. His shallow surroundings are nothing at all like simplicity. Finally he crosses the line in one brave and blind instant. The skeins of former levels he sheds like skins. He floats between viewpts, he can see anything he wants, and everything. A great bounty fills his eyes, with the promise of an infinite stream of visions to follow. Endless pictures in need of re-vision, separation, interpretation. Endless non-sequiturs of happenstance and dialogue, events, thoughts. On through the levels, on towards the end. at some point one hopes to mesh with the world, to slip quietly between the warp and woof, to live 'in between'.

"Maybe every tiny thing becomes clear in the end," he says. "Maybe I might know for sure."

"Maybe I'll find a true picture."
"Must I break a chain to build a chain?"
"Maybe the images never cease."
"Perhaps this smoke will never clear."

(but)

"Maybe this dream just goes on and on."

Paperbox
lower manhattan 100501

it's hard to describe what it's like here. the air wasn't so bad today.
they're keeping the dust down, big trucks spraying the streets night
and day. most days doesn't help more than a little bit, but even
that's something. all streets have cement barricades running the
edges of the sidewalks, backed w chain-link rent-a-fence/national
reserves in camouflage and cops on every corner. yesterday for first
time since we've been back, i went to see for myself. rode my bike
around the entire perimeter, stopping at all the blockades where the
tourists and curious locals w their cams gathered. down to a one too
stunned to snap. just staring...

liberty & broadway looking west, you could see them hosing down
the big pile. maiden lane & broadway, 1 block to the north, was the
most astoundingly fierce sight. some bldg i did not recognize, big
black hulking thing, had it's side pulled open to reveal the entire
structure, but was still standing. was that "four"? from the south
looking north on rector street you could survey the whole gaping cav-
ity, and see a lge part of one of the towers still standing. most beau-
tiful monument of all, the way it looked. i hope they leave it,
smoked up and ruined.

the streets at night are so empty. this is how tribeca used to be. it's
really humming with activity down here. all the cops and guardsmen
are doing a fantastic and courteous job. they have 'hero' status to
live up to, and it seems they sense it. everyone working seems to be
hauling ass to make it all happen, to patch the infrastructure seams
as quickly as possible and to keep the recovery operation moving.
verizon and con ed trucks, military vehicles and construction flat
beds carrying out huge girders all day long. under the arc lights the
work goes on all night, ignorant of the clock. the beams cast a bril-
liant column up through the air, filled w rising dust and smoke.

one image nobody got that first day was the shoes. no one got em,
in all the reporting. that afternoon just north of chambers & broad-
way there was a pile of shoes on the northwest corner, up against the
granite of the bldg there. mostly dusty black workers boots of some
sort—-lots of em—-but also some hi heels and stray other singles.
well more than a dozen pairs in all. what the hell were they doing
there? sitting poignant and mute, covered in fine ash and debris, to
both of us they somehow summed up the whole thing; the event, the
emotions, the angst. we noticed some other smaller piles as we
walked northwards, and over the next couple days i noticed other
piles of shoes, and lots of scattered singles and pairs on the streets...

the air quality down here, for residents and even more so for work-
ers, is decidedly not good. bottom line. no matter what the EPA and

others say. with small children, we are especially concerned. it just can't be good for them. funny how back in 'normal' life we'd toler-ate all the local spew of trucks and buses; now that the streets are pleasantly free of them we have a different menace in the air. it smells stinky a lot of the time, burning rubber stink, and yr eyes get red after awhile, throat scratchy and hoarse. i can't wear my con-tacts for more than half the day without itchy eyes. not many of the workers or military are wearing masks, and they're out in the air all day. can't be a good thing.

tonight after a reasonably normal dinner with friends across the park, i was belatedly hunting down a copy of the friday Times, w the weekend section. the newsstand by city hall was sold out, i walked across chambers to morgan's market on reade & hudson—no luck there either. returning home i tried a last, usually reliable stop—-a Times street-box just north of our place, on broadway just above chambers. the box was under some scaffolding, all dusty and pushed up against a lge green UPS mailbox. i had to yank at it to get at the front of it. bent down to check the date: friday, friday, c'mon be friday not thursday... but to my amazement if was sept 11. i could-nt believe it. of course we ran out that next morning and bought ALL the papers, and the next day and the next; and the magazines as they came, but the one we talked about was the paper from the 11th—i don't think many had time that day to read that one. this paper behind the glass was the last one in the box—i would've taken more had it not been—one paper from that morning still sitting in this box all these last 3 weeks. when that paper was put to bed, in the early morning hours of the 11th, while most of us slept peaceful-ly, the world was a different, more innocent place.

The American Desert,
photographs by Cynthia Connolly:

Lee Ranaldo, musician, writer, and visual artist, is an original member of the group Sonic Youth, formed in 1981 in New York City. They have recorded and performed throughout the world since that time. Among Lee's solo records are *East Jesus, Dirty Windows*—a collection of spoken texts with music—and *Amarillo Ramp (for Robert Smithson)*—pieces for the guitar. Recent CDs include Text of Light (with Alan Licht, DJ Olive, Christian Marclay, William Hooker and Ulrich Krieger) and Monsoon (with Roger Miller and William Hooker). Fall 2004 will see the release of a CD of his compositions for the theatre and film from the last three years. His books include *Bookstore, Road Movies* and *Jrnls80s*. A full-length book of writings on Moroccan travels is due in early 2005. His writings appear in the collections *Heights of the Marvelous, The Rolling Stone Beat Book* and *Verses that Hurt: The Poemphone Poets*. Recent visual work has been included in exhibitions at the Hayward Gallery in London, the Sydney Museum of Contemporary Art, the Kunsthalle Vienna and Gigantic Artspace in NYC. For more info check out http://www.sonicyouth.com/dotsonics/lee/

Cynthia Connolly grew up in Los Angeles. Moved to Washington, DC in 1981 as a young punk rocker. Graduated from the Corcoran School of Art with a BFA in Graphic Design in 1985. She published the Banned in DC book in 1988 with the help of Leslie Clague and Sharon Cheslow. During that time she booked bands and performances in the small alternative arts space called d.c. space, from 1986-1991. She also worked at Dischord Records doing advertising and promotion. In 1993, she started avidly doing photography again. The project "people from DC with their cars" for a zine called Speed Kills was the initial impetus. Since then, she has shown all over the world, with the "car" photos, but also newer photos of landscapes taken in 35mm black and white and also color photographs taken in color with the "half frame" format. Cynthia had collected postcards since she was young, and with the old cards as a reference, she designed a series of color half frame deckled edged cards that are both touristic in feel and very personal expressions of her travels. She recently published a set of cards in a printed box entitled, "the box of ice boxes". In 2002, she did an artist in residency at Harper's Ferry National Park. During her residency, she was accepted to Auburn University's Rural Studio program in Newbern, Alabama. She quit her job at Dischord, and went full time an 'outreacher', working on many projects. Her final project was supported by the Alabama State Council on the Arts and the National Endowment for the Arts. Upon returning to the DC area in the summer of 2003, she won a grant from Arlington County to document the Old Timey and Bluegrass musicians who perform in a park in Northern Virginia. The summer of 2004 brought her where she is today, hired by Arlington County as the county's art gallery manager. For more info check out http://www.cynthiaconnolly.com